1982

LIVING WITH DISTANCE

RALPH J. MILLS, JR.

Ralph J Mills Jr

LIVING

WITH

DISTANCE

Cover Photograph by Helen Mills

BOA EDITIONS • BROCKPORT • NEW YORK

Grateful acknowledgment is made to the editors of the following publications in which most of these poems appeared, sometimes in slightly different versions: *The American Poetry Review, Ascent, Banyan Press Anthology, Big Moon, Chicago Review, Crazy Horse, Dacotah Territory, Descant, Ironwood, Midwest Quarterly, Mississippi Valley Review, Moons and Lion Tailes, New England Review, New Letters, Northeast, Poem, Quarterly West, Seems, Slow Loris Reader, Spoon River Quarterly, Uzzano, Westigan Review.*

"The Door" reprinted by permission from *New England Review*, Vol. I, No. 2 (Winter 1978).

Printed at the Visual Studies Workshop.
Photographs by Helen Harvey Mills.
Distributed by The Book Bus, 31 Prince St., Rochester, N.Y.
Typeset by Advertising and Marketing Graphics

BOA Editions
Publisher: A. Poulin, Jr.
92 Park Avenue
Brockport, N.Y. 14420

Publication of this book was made possible in part with the assistance of a grant from the Literature Programs of the National Endowment for the Arts, a federal agency in Washington, D.C., and of the New York State Council on The Arts.

ISBN 0-918526-17-5 Cloth
　　　 0-918526-18-3 Paper

First Edition: May, 1979

For Michael Anania & Laurence Lieberman

ALSO BY RALPH J. MILLS, JR.

POETRY
Door to the Sun, The Baleen Press, 1974.
A Man to His Shadow, Juniper Books, 1975.
Night Road/Poems, The Rook Press, 1978.

CRITICISM
Theodore Roethke, University of Minnesota Press, 1963.
Contemporary American Poetry, Random House, 1965.
Richard Eberhart, University of Minnesota Press, 1966.
Edith Sitwell, Wm. B. Eerdmans, 1966.
Kathleen Raine, Wm. B. Eerdmans, 1967.
Creation's Very Self, Texas Christian University Press, 1969.
Cry of the Human, University of Illinois Press, 1975.

EDITED
On the Poet and His Craft: Selected Prose of Theodore Roethke,
     University of Washington Press, 1965.
Selected Letters of Theodore Roethke, University of Washington
     Press, 1968.
The Notebooks of David Ignatow, The Swallow Press, 1973.

CONTENTS

I

II

III

I

As I Breathe

The exposed branches and trunks
of two dead birches
glow,
pale ghosts from the shrubbery.

It's so dark —
again today the sky's gray wing
has folded down over the fields:
a headlong wind churns leaves
and rain explodes
in the brown river, the reeds.

Alone, I think as I breathe
of the body's fragile thin stone,
the face
closed tight as a shell,
the damp shadow of footprints
among clumps of grass.

Clouds

The moon has gone hiding —
nights fill up
with clouds
sagging damply onto
the roof.

And this dream of
yourself —
a feather falls
through the air of
a darkened room,
it never
stops falling . . .

When you wake
the ceiling stretches
above you,
pale, grainy white —
the painted body
of a cloud.

Shapes

The shapes of winter branches
lift and fall,
their undulant sea sway
stripped of green.

In late afternoon light
a small vase on the window sill —
closed dead roses,
brown, yellow streaking the leaves,
stems curling over,
weighted
like mourners' bent heads.

Darkness paints the glass:
a face swims there,
cold, silvery,
and staring as if risen to the surface
with lips parted for breath
or to shape some unanswerable question.

The Voices

Dreaming, I find the corridor,
my feet already in motion,
shadow grazing the whitewashed wall.

Outside night winds are flaying
vacant oaks and elms —
blue ghostly snow smothers their roots.

This town I grew up in, and left;
it sleeps like death,
streets black with ice curve through ravines.

But I can't help myself, pulled down a hall
by voices, knife-edged, hysterical —
my parents' marriage music, years past.

The open door, the room:
man and woman, almost knee to knee,
bent in anger.

Sensing me, they drop into silence,
turn as one faces I've never seen,
expressionless as the snow.

Roads, miles beyond now, I cross frozen fields
lit by a plum-colored moon;
bitter air knocks my forehead,
distances stretch nowhere, to the dream's end.

Down

This afternoon the crabapple trees inclined
their branches to the wind,
the knotted twigs still erect.

I woke at dawn
out of a dream that ended in tears,
a lost face,
the blankets clinging to me like wet earth.

Another year's dropped away
somewhere.
The hand in the dream couldn't hold on.

Night shoves through the trees again.
Below my window
the street lays down its narrow length
under a half-moon's gray unblinking eye.

Near Stonington

Damp heat films the skin,
a blurred sunlight like sluggish water
lapping the trees.

Gulls sweep off the stones
soaking in estuaries
and beat their way
through nets of dead air.

Always other lives —
they cross the horizon of daydreams,
as if my hand could unlock
any door.

Passing an old red barn
by the crossroads,
one that sags into its shadow,
I want to step in
without looking back from the dark.

Chelsea Churchyard

Crowded gravestones,
brothers, sisters in silence,
lean together and touch.

Walling the church's stained bulk
as it weathers another century,
they're ignorant how wind and rain
have whitened their thin shoulders
like a January snow.

Given away, names, stones,
grain after grain,
they need no one, nothing
but to be
where their shadows meet.

A Bridge

for Maurice English

The clouds today are streaked
with pale wash, a water color sky
the sun burns occasional holes through,
which don't last,
fire fading quickly in late September's air.

This afternoon
the long exhalation of beginning autumn,
single season of my poems
even when snow sweeps their pages
or June blazes gold
at the tips of uncut grass.

"A vision, if only of sorrow,"
a friend writes,
"to make a memorial of it."

The attempt, exactly.
Driving a deserted road toward the Des Plaines,
oaks, elms, maples, birches in a wall
and arching overhead.
The green tunnel leads to the river:
silver painted steel beams ahead
gleaming from the burst of rainfall.
A bridge:
words held together to sustain
in the pauses of breath what's departing
this minute, the next;
wind constant and fierce,
the stream rushing past underneath.

In the Night Air

The moon swings its sickle.
high over Sante Fe,
harvesting a black sky.

Winter climbs to the poplars' tips,
it's scrubbing juniper bark
behind the houses.

Torn through mountain passes,
wind rakes the ditches.
The highway north to Taos
gleams in moonlight
like a length of frozen string.

Flowers on spaded earth,
blown dry grass,
and above the white stones
remembered names
turning,
turning in the night air.

11/13/76

C. D. H.

High bare branches of elm
at four o'clock
splayed motionless in the sun's amber,
beyond trees and cemetery wall
a thread of smoke
curls into blue air.

Above us, foraging birds cry out,
wheel in the cold light,
sweeping over acres of graves.
We stand in clumps
or alone,
in our dark clothes bodiless almost
as shadows.

An hour ago, in church,
I saw your grandchild pick
from the casket quilted with flowers
a single petal
and hold to her lips this word
you left behind.

Stone or Pearl

"...a white stone in the well's depth
one memory lies within me." — *Anna Akhmatova*

Morning mist turns to rain,
a chill breath
flows out of the soaked grasses,
the pools beneath trees.

If I bury my face in a quilt,
away from the window's faint light,
with eyes closed,
I'll look down into deep
lapping water.

A stone or pearl shivers there
among the currents,
nacreous,
liquid silver, pearl blue,
or white
and shadowless.

Who can touch us now
where we meet in this glimmering
of your life in mine,
the years' secretion —
my memory, your death?

A Sun

I leave bed early —
the caul of dreams has shivered
and torn —
hearing window shade,
curtains
like wings in unison
slap against glass.

Dawn is lifting again,
leaner, grayer.
Today
less light pools in the alleys,
climbs vinelike up walls.

Under the screen of
turning leaves
tree limbs shine dully,
firm as iron.

A photograph on the desk —
your face
fixed above mine:

we are lit by
a sun
gone down forty years.

The Whisper

Out of sleep I come back,
it seems always,
to morning light on the elms, their leaves
poised as if listening,
to the young ash at the corner
that hovers in a green cloud.

Heat has thickened the air,
today the lake lies flat out, a sheet
of burning glass
under the sky's cornflower blue.

Trees and bird cries, the day's tasks,
familiar streets
running in the same directions.

What did it mean
when I woke, hours before dawn,
to the mind's whisper —
gray, darkening there at the center,
the edges,
the road spilling away in rain
like a flooded stream,
darker
and darker the heavy branches, the leaves'
tight net,
and the way home?

Here

Here the day opens on heat haze,
the buildings lost in it, leaves glittering
as they thrust out like tongues
to taste the damp sunlight.

Sadness of our bodies, our lives.
When it's quiet you can hear the bones clicking,
anxious for the ground.

I turn from the mirror, seeing my father's face
again in mine, tired of the deceit,
of my days unfolding into air, the same words,
traps of emptiness yawning underneath.
The table's edge drops off in space.

Almost Easter and the cherry tree outside lights
its small pink fires;
lilies, mums, azalea plants fill windows.
The risen Christ, is he here —
in the sun burning a gold fringe on thunderheads
blowing east over the city,
in the shadow of an old woman kneeling at prayer,
in the faint breath that crosses our lips as we sleep?

On the wall downstairs there's a Harry Callahan
photograph: three white stones
bedded in dark grass.
Sometimes I stare until the glass dissolves
and I've stepped through,
the tall blades springing back after I pass,
and I lie down so I'm touching
one stone or another lightly
with fingertips,
and being here, don't look ahead or behind.

Walking

Orange, yellow, violet: the wildflowers
draw up from sand on thin stems,
unfolding petals
to drain the light, the sky's blue gaze.

Barrel cactus lays a stunted shadow
across my path, and the ocotillo, "thorn of Christ,"
tangles its spiked branches,
twisting a red blossom
from each tip.

The day's bright wing spreads:
not even noon and everything shimmers,
quicksilver in the heat.
Just south, Camelback's humped mountain
rises, changing color,
purple to rust to green.

A mourning dove cries somewhere near,
among the leaves,
it calls me back twenty years —
a skein of memory and death hangs
for a moment on the air.

Walking further, I cross a road,
watch how it climbs foothills a mile
or more away, the tarred surface
relentless as the perfect white band
dividing its middle.

25

Like Them

I

A slight wind is waking the leaves
to an erratic dance. Sunlight
flecks the grass: spaces
of yellow, of green
darken as shadows reel over them.

Crossing a burnt-out stretch of park,
I feel through my shoes
the coarse blades.
The wind stills now along the branches,
a bird or brisk animal
drawn to rest.

II

A long placid glass, the lagoon
remembers nothing —
not the cast lines of men
fishing,
not a rowboat's wrinkled wake
or the clouds' passage. Only
the willows lean over here
and stay. Like them, I've aged
another year in this mirror.

III
I think of a dream a few weeks ago
which promised so much —
In my house
I ran to answer your knock on the door.
Everyone there was waiting
for you to walk back
from years of death.

But at my touch the door
was an empty window, rain-streaked
and filling up with the new day's
thin bodiless light.

Back Again

A bird whose name I don't know
calls out
from the green paradise of elms
slowly aging
a cry harsh and lonely as a whistling freight.

I turn on the blade of his voice
and spread wing,
under the cloud and shadow of flight.

A red seam of light opening edges along
the horizon
gives my life back again as if it were mine,
bobbing high on its string
above the broken crests of lake water.

II

Angel of Death

After a woodcut by Leonard Baskin

Don't bother,
you'll lock windows, doors
for nothing
when you see me
standing at dusk
tall among the trees
across the burnt summer grass,
myself a piece of darkness,
a deep stain on the air.

Chin and lips splashed red,
teeth ground to points,
my gut still sags,
a sack loose with hunger.
I'm dangerous as lava
snaking down a mountain.

I'll make your form mine
in the end.
Watch how I mold you
as you vanish on my tongue.
Behind me
you'll grow into memories,
columns of dust
swept toward the sky.

On bitter nights of ice
my feathers rattle
like weathered armor,
but my feet move in silence.
I know every road.

From me you win fear,
a bottomless sea
in the pool of your lamplight,
the key of a gate
to starless space.
My jaws swing on their hinges,
crush life after life.
Eating them all,
I never live.

The Last Word

After an Imogen Cunningham Photograph
of Theodore Roethke

You sit down in shade here;
the sun still warming your knees,
feeding rough grass, weed.
You pose also, squinting, tired.
Climbing's heavy, many falls,
but your feet are clouds, and dance.
Where you stop, back to wall,
leaning against your initial like a stump,
an eye reads portent.
Whose hand and finger slide
from the jagged lightning crack in stone?
They point a route for you: bleached highways,
cutting snow, the moon fired with another life,
while God strips your bark, nails the bone.
And it comes out song.

Now you get up, the finger hovers, insistent,
whitewashed angel of dark laws.
The road winds north, four years,
crosses to an island, a pool.
There you dive,
and give its water your last word.

Night Vigil

After Philippe Jaccottet

Make no sound here
this room belongs to the dead
Lift your candle
and he moves further off

Stop by the door
to raise your voice
a little
speaking words that light
small torches
along the path he's taken

Those who remain
praying
beneath the snow's white burden
will hear small birds
at daybreak
carry their voices on

34

Said in Whispers

Variations on a poem by Jules Supervielle

Don't be frightened
Close both eyelids slowly
They become white shells
shining on the long sloping
beach of the cheekbones
under the shadow
of the nose's sharp cliff
where the endless ocean begins

The heart must follow
the course of its own will
which is to stop
If it hammers like a clock
that is for its pleasure alone
listening as if buried
in the tall grass of a hillside
watching the sea and
the lines of clouds driven
by the wind

The hands lie straight out
They are motionless, translucent
two barges carved from icy light
waiting for the moon
to call them back on the tide

The forehead is naked
vulnerable as a sleeping child's
but cold
leaning away into darkness
like a deserted church
or the square of a city
everyone has left

Night in Me

Variations on a poem by Jules Supervielle

When night comes, I wait
for the second one, deeper and blacker,
to rise inside me,
a shoreless ocean with two skies
sliding together above.
Strange, but I'm used to this —
being alone in a dinghy, pulling oars
through the dark between nights
no one can tell apart.

                 If I stop,
look around, there's nothing to see,
just myself, a point
on the surface where the small wreath
of my breath hangs
distant in the salt air.
I listen to the slap of oars; lulled
by waves scrubbing the hull, I keep
circling quietly.

Night touches me all over.
Sometimes I think of the depths
beneath —
what moves through them?
They must darken further down, like sleep;
as you sink, silver bubbles ascend
in a stream . . .
then coral, grass, sand, bones:
the sea's floor.

I belong to both nights:
one shadow spreads its wing
across my shoulders.
Behind me, the boat's wake vanishes,
luminous
with stars that glitter there
and drown.

Sun

Variations on a poem by Pierre Reverdy

Who was it passing by
who has already gone
someone who left a patch of shade
behind I can almost touch
in the air

Who left a sigh too
a small breath drifting free
visible as a cloud
which suddenly enters the window
changing the landscape of your room

Still my house is empty
my hands beat at the wind
without music
the trees are stripping for winter

The street outside
departs for its own destination
I'm watching it lean on the curve
but seeing a lone path of sunlight
move far off
like a lover's gaze that makes distances green

Above and Below

Variations on a poem by Pierre Reverdy

The storm gets closer
Rain sways among the trees
their trunks glisten like the newly born
Over a pool's swollen eye
branches poise motionless, attentive.

From your feet water spreads a path
it bends up sharply, a refraction of light
thrust into the sky

              Someone leaves that way
someone always leaving, who closes a door
You watch as he rises
and is air lifted through a crown of shadows
above the crested elms

            What falls
Rain, returning tears given each day everywhere
to the ground, mist of our soil
drawn between the parted lips of a cloud

              Who laughs
No one You are listening to sighs, to someone's
breath with cleft tongue, who doesn't speak
and will not come down

Signs

After Pierre Reverdy

When all backs are turned
I stare at the wall
Someone's voice in my ear
A hand on the windowpane
And another outside
Are the same
The sun tries to break in
A bird in the alley takes off
Screeching
But a cry drifts down
From above
I should know it
A man who climbs the steep sky
I stand listening
He's naked
His body too
Under changing clouds
Between blue air
And the black storm

Variation on du Bouchet

After "Équerre"

Here the air's so thin even grass
draws into its roots

Nothing more than a thread of glass
the stream motionless in its furrow
glistening
white as a fish bone

A cloud pauses
in flight
the ground darkens under it
purple, bruised

ravaged by the sudden shadow
overhead

A Poem for Louise Glück

It is dusk there, I know, the horizon
thinning into gray strands.
Vermont's bird of autumn waits
in the maple branches, ready
to sweep the hills.

This is yours —
the weather down among the stones,
the reeds' sharp whisper across a blackening pond,
stands of pine guarding the distance.

All day you move from room to room,
tend the child, write a few letters
to the world outside.
You chop lettuce and slice bread, uncork
a bright wine for the one who might
come to your table.

Staring out on the water,
you're not surprised to see
an August moon like a mottled orange
break through its surface
and speak. You haven't forgotten
how voices call, faces tremble
each evening in the pond's ripples:
they're not only the moon's familiars.

You've stayed a long time —
there's nowhere else.
When you climb the wood porch,
walk quietly in at last
toward the one ring of lamplight,
blank paper stares,
the desk's rubbed grain shines.

I listen to the late wind stir
for a thousand miles:
long past midnight leaves are strumming
under your fingers.

Four Songs for John Knoepfle

I
The new month begins
its slow ascension
rain clouds
lengthening their shadow
across the map

White ash, maple, oak
shiver
in the wind's grip
an aspen ruffles
green and silver plumage
When the lake
kicks up
the gulls rise

II

Two weeks ago
riding downstate I saw
in the turned
seeded black fields
crabapple and cherry
scattering bloom
over islands of grasses

Scrubbed like coral
a daytime moon leaned down
attentively
from the mediterranean blue

III
A man kneels to the ground
to drag up weed
clear away dead twigs
and pack the dirt
around stems
his back arches as the sky
above him
bends
toward its horizons

At night by his window
listening to rain
the solitary voices of so many trees
wind threading through the grass
he may speak
hesitantly among them

IV
Thin as leaves
in this dream we float
sometimes
near to one another
buoyed on an exuberance
of light
as if always
a deep water moved under
and about us, stirring
its hidden muscles
like the sea

A Last Poem

Variations on a poem by Robert Desnos
for H., N., J., & B.

Dreaming of you so long,
so hard, I have exhausted my sleep
until it is empty, an open palm
in which the rain falls

Walking so far,
I have thinned out all the roads
to a single line, narrower than string,
a horizon no foot can grip

Always talking on the way,
I have ground syllables to dust in my teeth
Birds peck at the grains of my alphabet
I draw breath deeply,
and quiet drifts in, a mist from the sea

Loving even your shadows so much,
I have seen them as one,
held them so close that now
when I must leave
they will nest forever in my eye

Finally I will be only shadow,
passing into a shadow company
as evening light on trees or a wall
enters the night's gradual tide

But you will not lose me,
a shade of such longing, I shall remain
in your lives, waiting like a sentinel
along their routes with gentle darkness
to touch over and over the sunlit days.

48

III

Soon

An afternoon driving
through familiar towns.
The road loses itself,
coins of light shower down
on the asphalt
from dense swaying branches.

There is a life no one lives
among these streets,
in the smallest houses —
out of desire
you call it yours.

But tonight the towns have
moved years off
into sleep —
they won't waken for you.

Soon the rain will begin.
A wind you remember hums
stridently
behind the walls,
tests flaking brick
and whistles through a chink

You don't understand anything
Nothing No you don't No

Living with Distance

I

November nights lengthen out,
frost stars the blackened leaves.
Now a swollen moon pulls loose
its shoulder
from clouds above the lake's
glittering rim, the city
hung in chains of light.
On the wall of my house
vines, stripped for winter, rattle
and snap like wire.

II

A cold wind whirls at the mind's
corners — disconsolate, it whistles
in the tangled strands of grass
low wordless tunes
of what we've missed.

III

Living with distance,
with miles, with seasons and death,
everything moving stubbornly
in a stream like the clouds tonight,
I live
with a dream of the print of my hands
on your body,
of yours on mine,
of what once always was possible —
and what never was.

For Years

I
At midday
sparrows gossip on
the window ledge,
wisps of cirrus
drifting overhead, passing
beneath a shredded
collar of moon.

October declines —
a scrawl of blackened pods
hangs from the locust;
grasses arch, stiff
with frost; sleet,
crossing the plains,
beats its tattoo.

II
My father used to nap
in his chair after work
and a long drive: sunlight
paled in the west
windows, threw fading patches
on the rug.

For years I knew
why he did this,
and have done the same,
slipping down
wave after wave
where the trough opens
wide below,

not anxious ever
to rise again, emptied,
breathless,
and find only the room —
single window, door,
a tree outside heavy with snow.

In February

I
This snow, sun-dazzled
by three days' thaw,
the crystal whiteness
drawn up into air, has left
only damp shapes
to print the knots of withered grass.

II
An electric saw rasps through
the afternoon's iron gray.
On the corner, elm limbs, branches
lie scattered about
the stump, its raw splinters
bristling like quills.

III
Sudden icy wind slaps at the ash
tree's thin frame; a shred of moon
hangs above clouds rushing east
over the lake.

Inside, I spread a hand
on the table, my palm
opening into slopes and ravines
of a weathered topography.

Going nowhere, I turn
in the night to reach among memories
that come apart, fade,
not caring
if they're no more than clouds
and belong to someone else's life.

Winter's End

Winter's end: sparrows
clatter from the hedge;
rain turns to snow, then
back again.
        A last
hard wind shuddering
against houses, veers south.

I drift, season
into season. Children
who rise like clouds
around me, changing shape,
fly off in the distance.

On the phone, someone talks
of loneliness, of what's
left of life — "You think
I am strong," she says,
longing even
for the pain of her bad marriage.

Evening spills through
tangled branches, the street
dances faintly now
with moonlight —

I'm fumbling, loose on its path,
growing older,
but helpless almost as the child
I was
and shy of the dark.

March

At night
you speak in my
sleep, more palpable
than the restless
spring weather,
shaken branches of
ailanthus or
rain-slick streets.
Your face blooms
in dream disguise
on a pillow's
slope, cheeks
full, russet
as two apples
against snow.

I bend to listen,
touch —
and find you
are dying, while
still your speech
flows, calm,
unhalting, a stream
that lilts
into song. Smiling
only for death's
pleasure, you
wave me away.

Weightless,
I am a cloud
lifted silently
from you, to forget
your words
while March rains
wash the night
outside, and green,
purple, crimson,
ochre,
hard as knots,
buds erupt on every
twig and
claim the air.

The Door

for Brett

In a tangle of sheets
I beach
on sleeplessness, hearing
time click hesitate click
seeing
my watch dial flicker
like a distant city,

and thinking myself
past sleep or rest
suddenly I dream —

A simple panelled door,
beyond it rigid shadow,
gray, opaque as unmarked stone,
where nothing moves,
looks out,
lives —

Emptiness invites me, this
curtain of ash —
my skin is chilled
to frost,
sweats a dew.

Who can stare it down?
I try:
but then call out a name.

Rounded into a cloud,
the face of my small daughter
slips near,
and we ride toward
morning's orange
uplifting eye.

As Now

In tonight's deepening
blue air
the moon lifts
full face
over brick walls, a roof's edge
its distant touch
cool as china plate
on my skin
like the hand that used to
clasp mine a moment
when I drifted
as now
into the first sleep

The Second Life

Somewhere past twelve
driven
from the wilderness of sleep
I get up
to drink cold water
that foams through pipes
glitters in a cup
out of the lake's dark churning

Wind skids across roofs
the streetlamp nods loosely
like a damaged flower
clouds come unstuck
and the moon
empties stolen brightness
on spring branches
beaded green
by a day's sudden heat

Maple, elm, ash
cherry and oak are unfolding
into knobby wings
above ground their roots hug

Returned to the familiar
this window and room
I lie back to dream again
and hear my dead father breathe
in his sleep
under budding leaves
his breath the gliding of air
over tips of new grass
where now as I listen
the second life already
has begun

At the Middle

This afternoon, dense, breathless —
my mouth closed, eyes, forehead
in a dream of suffocation.

It's late summer at the middle of my life:
nothing moves
but the sluggish river below, walled in
by bushes and rotting trunks.

Weeks ago in London, I walked the parks,
picking up dried beech leaves, looking for poems.
The city like a great body pulsed, sparkled with heat;
on the Thames boats floating in a mirage,
dust scuffed along circular paths.

By the Des Plaines again, I can hear
the first evening wind start to rustle.
I step
where the leaves' darkness falls.
These old weighted trees — who gives them a look,
fingers their rough bark cooling from the day?
Overhead, one after another, they're shaken
from stillness,
and I reach out to touch them, thinking strangely
of doors, flowers, hands — anything at all
that opens, unfurls, blooms on the air.

In This Hour

Air clings, moist as peeled fruit
from the afternoon heat —

I am watchful, dreaming.

A wind ripples ivy
outside the window,
spears of grass thrust
flame-tipped
even as the light goes.

Almost full, the moon
coats roofs a tarnished silver,
sharpens the edges of leaves
until they gleam.

River 'of the plains'
your wrist of moonswept brown water
curves into thought, distant
and thin.

In this hour
I wish for nothing
but to be filled with what I can see

and to walk to the half-open door
in the air ahead.

Now Again

*"These changes cry out for a life that
does not change."*
　　　　　　　　　—Louis Simpson

Now in the chill dusk
spring approaches.
It's riding a wind flung
along highways, the concrete
speckled with rain,
clouds changing shape
in dream figures overhead.

I can't turn away from these thoughts,
from the dead at each shoulder,
so full of useless longing for them,
for what the hand can't grasp
even when it's here.

Papers rustle on a table.
I drive black ink tracks over their margins:
the words lifted back into air
assemble a life,
the one I keep walking out of.

Again a beginning: windows, doors;
outside, the quick yellow bloom;
branches gleaming faintly, wreathed
with budding leaves.
Further off,
the streaked phosphorous roads
run everywhere, fate-lines,
threads pulled together and knotted
across the horizon.

Now again the threatened heart,
a blood fruit on its stem,
sways in the wind.

A Note

With the exception of "Signs" and "Night Vigil," which are free versions, the poems derived from the French in the second section are what I have called "variations" on the original texts. In each instance I have expanded or enlarged upon the original poems, using their imagery and themes as a starting point. The resulting poems can be read separately in English but have their foundation and source in the works of the French poets.

The texts I have used are as follows: for "Sun," *Modern European Poetry*, ed. Willis Barnstone (New York, 1966) in Anna Balakian's translation; for "Above and Below" and "Signs," Pierre Reverdy: *Sources du Vent* (Paris, 1971); for "Said in Whispers" and "A Last Poem," *The Penguin Book of French Verse 4: The Twentieth Century*, ed. Anthony Hartley (Baltimore, 1966); for "Variation on du Bouchet," *Botteghe Oscure Reader*, ed. George Garrett (Middletown, Conn., 1974); for "Night in Me," *Selected Writings of Jules Supervielle* (New York, 1967); for "Night Vigil," Philippe Jaccottet: *Poésie 1946-1967* (Paris, 1971). I have retained the original titles, translated, except in the case of André du Bouchet's poem and Supervielle's "Said in Whispers," which bears an original title in English of "Whisper in Agony."

68

Living with Distance has been issued in a first edition of 1200 copies, seven hundred and fifty of which are in paper and four hundred copies are in cloth. An additional 50 copies have been specially bound in quarter-cloth and French papers over boards by Gene Eckert; ten copies, numbered I-X, have been signed and include a poem in holograph by Ralph J. Mills, Jr.; twenty-six copies have been lettered A-Z and signed by the poet; fourteen copies, numbered i-xiv and signed by the poet, have been retained for presentation purposes.

Ralph J. Mills, Jr. was born in 1931. He graduated from Lake Forest College in 1954, received an M.A. from Northwestern University in 1956 and a Ph.D. from there in 1963. He has taught at Northwestern, the University of Chicago and, since 1965, at the University of Illinois, Chicago Circle, where he is Professor of English. Mr. Mills has published two major collections of essays, critical monographs on Theodore Roethke, Richard Eberhart, Edith Sitwell and Kathleen Raine, and he has edited Roethke's letters and prose as well as the *Notebooks* of David Ignatow. His poems have appeared in a wide variety of journals and in three previous chapbook collections. He is married, with three children, and lives in Chicago.